Consultants: David Olson, Director of Undergraduate Studies, and
Tamara Olson, Associate Professor, Department of Mathematical Sciences,
Michigan Technological University

Where are the kittens?
These kittens are
in the basket.

This kitten is out of the basket.

Where are the birds?
These birds are
in the nest.

This bird is
out of the nest.

Where are the lions?
These lions are
on the tree.

This lion is behind the tree.

Where is the bird?
This bird is
above the flower.

This bird is below the flower.

Where are the cows?
These cows are
near the barn.

These cows are far from the barn.

Where are the monkeys?
These monkeys are
on a branch.

This monkey is under the branch.

Where are the penguins?
These penguins are
on the ice.

These penguins are
in the water.

Where is the owl?